WHEN *the* NIGHT
DOTH
MEET *the* NOON

Poems by John Keats

John Constable   Sunset Study of Hampstead

WHEN *the* NIGHT DOTH MEET *the* NOON

Poems by John Keats

SELECTED AND WITH AN INTRODUCTION BY PAMELA TODD

PAVILION

For my Brothers, With Love

First published in Great Britain in 1996 by
PAVILION BOOKS LIMITED
26 Upper Ground, London SE1 9PD

A CIP catalogue record for this book is available from the British Library

ISBN 1 85793 639 6

Designed by David Fordham
Typeset in Helvetica Bold and Garamond Light by SX Composing Ltd, Rayleigh
Printed and bound in Italy by Graphicom

2 4 6 8 10 9 7 5 3 1

This book may be ordered by post direct from the publisher.
Please contact the Marketing Department. But try your bookshop first.

Contents

When *the* Night Doth Meet *the* Noon

'I think I shall be among the English poets after my death,' Keats wrote to his brother, George, in October 1818. It was a remarkably defiant statement made by a young man of twenty-two, reeling from the hostile critical reception of his long poem, *Endymion: a Poetic Romance*. He had no money, little recognition beyond a small circle of friends, his new, ambitious poem 'Hyperion' was not developing as he had hoped and he could not seem to shake off a persistent sore throat. Nevertheless he went on with 'strength and determination' to write all his major poems, including his great odes 'To a Nightingale' and 'On a Grecian Urn', as well as his lovely, mellow 'To Autumn', which remain some of the most widely read and best-loved lines in English.

Keats had a great gusto for life and, despite what he himself described as 'a horrid morbidity of temperament', outwardly at least he appeared to his friends as lively and attractive, with a generous sense of humour (he was much given to punning) and tremendous energy. He also had extraordinary powers of concentration, an ability to immerse himself in and sensuously identify with a subject (a process he

Joseph Severn   John Keats Reading at Wentworth Place

termed 'negative capability') and a mature and ambitious vision of what he hoped to achieve through his writing. 'Poetry,' he wrote to John Taylor, his publisher, in February 1818, 'should surprise by a fine excess . . . Its touches of Beauty should never be half way . . . If Poetry comes not as naturally as Leaves to a tree it had better not come at all.'

Keats's career as a poet had begun relatively late and ended tragically early. His first poem, 'Imitation of Spenser', was written in 1814 in a burst of enthusiasm occasioned by a reading of Spenser's *The Fairie Queene* that had gone on into the night. He was eighteen and at that time training to be a doctor. His last poem, a few lines possibly addressed to his fiancé, Fanny Brawne, was written in December 1820, when he was dying slowly from tuberculosis in Italy, an arduous sea journey away from those he loved most. Into those scant half a dozen years Keats succeeded in compressing as much change and growth as most writers experience in a lifetime. His total output is not large, but his work became a seminal influence for other poets, notably Tennyson in the 1830s and a decade later for the Pre-Raphaelite Brotherhood, who drew inspiration from poems like 'The Eve of St Agnes' and 'La Belle Dame Sans Merci' and ensured that Keats's reputation grew steadily in the years after his death. Today his reputation as a major poet is assured as the extraordinary brilliance, spontaneity and freshness of his poems continue to speak to new generations across the years and amply fulfil his ambition to be 'the Poet of the human heart'.

Keats's brief life is well documented. We know that he was born at the Swan and Hoop livery stables, which his father managed, in the City of London on 31 October 1795. At eight, he and his younger brother were sent to school in Enfield, ten miles from London, where a liberal education was offered by the gentle headmaster, John Clarke, to the sons of families who were in trade. He was a pugnacious little boy, sensitive about his lack of stature (even as a man Keats measured only three-quarters of an inch over five feet) but warm and well-liked. However, after only a year at school, the first of a sequence of sadnesses that were to punctuate his life and shape his poetic temperament occurred: his father died in a riding accident and his mother, young, impulsive and in trouble, married unwisely again within two months, lodging the four Keats children (of whom John at nine was the eldest) with her mother. His genial grandfather died the following year leaving behind an 'obscure' will full of vague phrasing, which resulted in hardship and complications for the family. Complications that were only finally resolved in 1888, sixty-seven years after Keats's death, when it was discovered that a sizeable sum of money, which would have kept him from poverty and probably have enabled him to marry his beloved Fanny Brawne, resided uncollected in Chancery. His mother's marriage was not a success and she returned home, already suffering from the fatal family tendency to tuberculosis, from which, in 1810, she died. Keats, who was only fourteen, had nursed her through the winter and his sensitive and passionate nature was devastated by her death. More was to come. Four years later his grandmother died and four years after that his much cherished brother, Tom. By now all Keats's boyish robustness had disappeared, for the nursing of Tom had severely weakened his own fragile health.

For a time Keats had combined his medical studies at Guy's Hospital with his burgeoning career as a poet, but an early mentor, Leigh Hunt, 'sealed his fate' and ensured that Keats 'gave himself up completely to Poetry' in December 1816 when Hunt included Keats's poem 'On Looking into Chapman's Homer' in an article in the *Examiner* entitled, 'Young Poets', which also introduced the work of Shelley and Reynolds. Keats published his first collection the following year and *Endymion* the year after that. In the space of a single, glorious year – 1819 – he produced an astonishing amount of verse, including all his odes. Some have suggested that love was the spur, for Keats, after a few amorous adventures, had met his vivacious Hampstead neighbour, Miss Fanny Brawne, and fallen deeply in love. He first mentions her in a letter to his brother George on 16 December 1818:

> Mrs Brawne who took Brown's house for the Summer, still resides in Hampstead
> – she is a very nice woman – and her daughter senior is I think beautiful and
> elegant, graceful, silly, fashionable and strange – we have a little tiff now and then
> – and she behaves a little better, or I must have sheered off.

Keats thought she was a 'minx' and told her so. They became engaged in the autumn of 1819 and a third volume of poems was published in 1820, but it was to be his last, for already Keats was dying. On 3 February 1820, three days after he had bidden farewell to his last remaining brother, George, who was emigrating to America, he had a severe haemorrhage in the lungs. It occurred on the journey home from Liverpool when Keats, in an effort to save money, had been travelling, exposed to the raw cold, on top of the stagecoach. When he finally staggered home to his friend Charles Brown's house in Hampstead he was feverish. Brown persuaded him to go at once to bed but:

On entering the cold sheets, before his head was on the pillow, he slightly coughed and I heard him say, – 'that is blood from my mouth'. I went towards him; he was examining a single drop of blood on the sheet. 'Bring me the candle, Brown; and let me see this blood.' After regarding it steadfastly, he looked up in my face, with a calmness of countenance that I can never forget, and said – 'I know the colour of that blood; – it is arterial blood; – I cannot be deceived in that colour; – that drop of blood is my death-warrant; – I must die.'

Keats's doctors advised him that he would not survive a winter in England and so it was arranged that he should travel to Italy in the company of the painter Joseph Severn. The harsh sea crossing, however, taxed his failing strength and Keats was tormented by the thought that he might never see his 'sweet Fanny' again. In a letter to her he wrote:

'If I die,' said I to myself, 'I have left no immortal work behind me – nothing to make my friends proud of my memory – but I have loved the principle of beauty in all things, and if I had had the time I would have made myself remembered.'

The two young men took rooms in the Piazza di Spagna in Rome where, despite never quite losing his 'cheerful and elastic' frame of mind, Keats died on 23 February 1821 in Severn's arms. He was twenty-five years old. He was buried before daylight three days later in the Protestant Cemetery where the epitaph he had chosen – 'Here lies one whose name was writ in water' – was engraved on his tombstone.

The tragedy of so much promise, such *joie de vivre* and such capacity for love cut short sears the imagination still. Keats was born 200 years ago yet his poetry remains fresh to us today. His talent is a young man's but the subjects of life and love, truth and beauty, art and nature which he explored through his poetry are ageless and we can find in his rich, voluptuous rhythms answers that both compel and console. Unlike Wordsworth, who believed that poetry should be 'emotion recollected in tranquillity', Keats composed in the white heat of the moment, sometimes up to fifty lines a day, and his best work falls across the page like sunlight. He spoke frequently of a 'fever' that accompanied his creative moods, often preceded by the 'indolence' or 'drowsy numbness' he celebrates in his odes. He combined an unusual intensity of feeling with a perfect sense of the music of words and, in his sonnets and odes, he developed a tone of voice for thinking aloud in verse. Indeed, his best poems are rich self-communings through which his deep love of nature and extraordinary ability to lose himself in an empathetic identification with his subject – be it a nightingale or a grasshopper – shines out. His work was brave, ambitious and innovatory as he strived to transfer the nature of the external world into poetry. Writing of Byron he said, 'He describes what he sees – I describe what I imagine – Mine is the hardest task.'

PAMELA TODD 1996

I STOOD TIP-TOE UPON A LITTLE HILL,

The air was cooling, and so very still,
That the sweet buds which with a modest pride
Pull droopingly, in slanting curve aside,
Their scantly leav'd, and finely tapering stems,
Had not yet lost those starry diadems
Caught from the early sobbing of the morn.
The clouds were pure and white as flocks new shorn,
And fresh from the clear brook; sweetly they slept
On the blue fields of heaven, and then there crept
A little noiseless noise among the leaves,
Born of the very sigh that silence heaves:
For not the faintest motion could be seen
Of all the shades that slanted o'er the green.
There was wide wand'ring for the greediest eye,
To peer about upon variety;
Far round the horizon's crystal air to skim,
And trace the dwindled edgings of its brim;
To picture out the quaint, and curious bending
Of a fresh woodland alley, never ending;
Or by the bowery clefts, and leafy shelves,
Guess where the jaunty streams refresh themselves.
I gazed awhile, and felt as light, and free
As though the fanning wings of Mercury
Had play'd upon my heels: I was light-hearted,

And many pleasures to my vision started;
So I straightway began to pluck a posey
Of luxuries bright, milky, soft and rosy.

A bush of May flowers with the bees about them;
Ah, sure no tasteful nook would be without them;
And let a lush laburnum oversweep them,
And let long grass grow round the roots to keep them
Moist, cool and green; and shade the violets,
That they may bind the moss in leafy nets.

A filbert hedge with wild briar overtwined,
And clumps of woodbine taking the soft wind
Upon their summer thrones; there too should be
The frequent chequer of a youngling tree,
That with a score of light green brethren shoots
From the quaint mossiness of aged roots:
Round which is heard a spring-head of clear waters
Babbling so wildly of its lovely daughters
The spreading blue-bells: it may haply mourn
That such fair clusters should be rudely torn
From their fresh beds, and scattered thoughtlessly
By infant hands, left on the path to die.

William Turner of Oxford   Extensive Wooded Landscape with a Distant View of a Town

13

John Constable   SUMMER MORNING: DEDHAM FROM LANGHAM

Open afresh your round of starry folds,

Ye ardent marigolds!

Dry up the moisture from your golden lids,

For great Apollo bids

That in these days your praises should be sung

On many harps, which he has lately strung;

And when again your dewiness he kisses,

Tell him, I have you in my world of blisses:

So haply when I rove in some far vale,

His mighty voice may come upon the gale.

Here are sweet peas, on tip-toe for a flight:

With wings of gentle flush o'er delicate white,

And taper fingers catching at all things,

To bind them all about with tiny rings.

Linger awhile upon some bending planks

That lean against a streamlet's rushy banks,

And watch intently Nature's gentle doings:

They will be found softer than ring-dove's cooings.

How silent comes the water round that bend;

Not the minutest whisper does it send

To the o'erhanging sallows: blades of grass

Slowly across the chequer'd shadows pass.

Why, you might read two sonnets, ere they reach

To where the hurrying freshnesses aye preach

A natural sermon o'er their pebbly beds;

Where swarms of minnows show their little heads,

Staying their wavy bodies 'gainst the streams,

To taste the luxury of sunny beams

Temper'd with coolness. How they ever wrestle

With their own sweet delight, and ever nestle

Their silver bellies on the pebbly sand.

If you but scantily hold out the hand,

That very instant not one will remain;

But turn your eye, and they are there again.

The ripples seem right glad to reach those cresses,

And cool themselves among the em'rald tresses;

The while they cool themselves, they freshness give,

And moisture, that the bowery green may live:

So keeping up an interchange of favours,

Like good men in the truth of their behaviours.

Sometimes goldfinches one by one will drop

From low hung branches; little space they stop;

But sip, and twitter, and their feathers sleek;

Then off at once, as in a wanton freak:

Or perhaps, to show their black, and golden wings,

Pausing upon their yellow flutterings.

Extract from I STOOD TIP-TOE UPON A LITTLE HILL

As LATE I RAMBLED IN THE HAPPY FIELDS,

What time the sky-lark shakes the tremulous dew

From his lush clover covert; – when anew

Adventurous knights take up their dinted shields:

I saw the sweetest flower wild nature yields,

A fresh-blown musk-rose; 'twas the first that threw

Its sweets upon the summer: graceful it grew

As is the wand that queen Titania wields.

And, as I feasted on its fragrancy,

I thought the garden-rose it far excell'd:

But when, O Wells! thy roses came to me

My sense with their deliciousness was spell'd:

Soft voices had they, that with tender plea

Whisper'd of peace, and truth, and friendliness unquell'd.

Thomas Gainsborough ANNE SPENSER

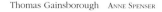

Early 19th Century School   LANDSCAPE

BARDS OF PASSION AND OF MIRTH,

Ye have left your souls on earth!
Have ye souls in heaven too,
Double lived in regions new?
Yes, and those of heaven commune
With the spheres of sun and moon;
With the noise of fountains wond'rous,
And the parle of voices thund'rous;
With the whisper of heaven's trees
And one another, in soft ease
Seated on Elysian lawns
Brows'd by none but Dian's fawns;
Underneath large blue-bells tented,
Where the daisies are rose-scented,
And the rose herself has got
Perfume which on earth is not;
Where the nightingale doth sing
Not a senseless, tranced thing,
But divine melodious truth;
Philosophic numbers smooth;
Tales and golden histories
Of heaven and its mysteries.

Thus ye live on high, and then
On the earth ye live again;
And the souls ye left behind you
Teach us, here, the way to find you,
Where your other souls are joying,
Never slumber'd, never cloying.
Here, your earth-born souls still speak
To mortals, of their little week;
Of their sorrows and delights;
Of their passions and their spites;
Of their glory and their shame;
What doth strengthen and what maim.
Thus ye teach us, every day,
Wisdom, though fled far away.

Bards of Passion and of Mirth,
Ye have left your souls on earth!
Ye have souls in heaven too,
Double-lived in regions new!

Ever let the Fancy roam,

Pleasure never is at home:

At a touch sweet Pleasure melteth,

Like to bubbles when rain pelteth;

Then let winged Fancy wander

Through the thought still spread beyond her:

Open wide the mind's cage-door,

She'll dart forth, and cloudward soar.

O sweet Fancy! let her loose;

Summer's joys are spoilt by use,

And the enjoying of the Spring

Fades as does its blossoming;

Autumn's red-lipp'd fruitage too,

Blushing through the mist and dew,

Cloys with tasting: What do then?

Sit thee by the ingle, when

The sear faggot blazes bright,

Spirit of a winter's night;

When the soundless earth is muffled,

And the caked snow is shuffled

From the ploughboy's heavy shoon;

When the Night doth meet the Noon

In a dark conspiracy

To banish Even from her sky.

Sit thee there, and send abroad,

With a mind self-overaw'd,

Fancy, high-commission'd: – send her!

She has vassals to attend her:

She will bring, in spite of frost,

Beauties that the earth hath lost;

She will bring thee, all together,

All delights of summer weather;

All the buds and bells of May,

From dewy sward or thorny spray;

All the heaped Autumn's wealth,

With a still, mysterious stealth:

She will mix these pleasures up

Like three fit wines in a cup,

And thou shalt quaff it: – thou shalt hear

Distant harvest-carols clear;

Rustle of the reaped corn;

Sweet birds antheming the morn:

And, in the same moment – hark!

'Tis the early April lark,

Or the rooks, with busy caw,

Foraging for sticks and straw.

Thou shalt, at one glance, behold

The daisy and the marigold;

John Linnell   THE WHITE COW

White-plum'd lillies, and the first
Hedge-grown primrose that hath burst;
Shaded hyacinth, alway
Sapphire queen of the mid-May;
And every leaf, and every flower
Pearled with the self-same shower.
Thou shalt see the field-mouse peep
Meagre from its celled sleep;
And the snake all winter-thin
Cast on sunny bank its skin;
Freckled nest-eggs thou shalt see
Hatching in the hawthorn-tree,
When the hen-bird's wing doth rest
Quiet on her mossy nest;
Then the hurry and alarm
When the bee-hive casts its swarm;
Acorns ripe down-pattering,
While the autumn breezes sing.

Oh, sweet Fancy! let her loose;
Every thing is spoilt by use:
Where's the cheek that doth not fade,
Too much gaz'd at? Where's the maid
Whose lip mature is ever new?

Where's the eye, however blue,
Doth not weary? Where's the face
One would meet in every place?
Where's the voice, however soft,
One would hear so very oft?
At a touch sweet Pleasure melteth
Like to bubbles when rain pelteth.
Let, then, winged Fancy find
Thee a mistress to thy mind:
Dulcet-eyed as Ceres' daughter,
Ere the God of Torment taught her
How to frown and how to chide;
With a waist and with a side
White as Hebe's, when her zone
Slipt its golden clasp, and down
Fell her kirtle to her feet,
While she held the goblet sweet,
And Jove grew languid. – Break the mesh
Of the Fancy's silken leash;
Quickly break her prison-string
And such joys as these she'll bring. –
Let the winged Fancy roam,
Pleasure never is at home.

TO SOME LADIES

WHAT THOUGH WHILE THE WONDERS OF NATURE EXPLORING,

    I cannot your light, mazy footsteps attend;

Nor listen to accents, that almost adoring,

    Bless Cynthia's face, the enthusiast's friend:

Yet over the steep, whence the mountain stream rushes,

    With you, kindest friends, in idea I muse;

Mark the clear tumbling crystal, its passionate gushes,

    In spray that the wild flower kindly bedews.

Why linger you so, the wild labyrinth strolling?

    Why breathless, unable your bliss to declare?

Ah, you list to the nightingale's tender condoling,

    Responsive to sylphs, in the moon-beamy air.

Joseph Mallord William Turner   THE EVENING STAR

'Tis morn, and the flowers with dew are yet drooping,

    I see you are treading the verge of the sea:

And now! ah, I see it – you just now are stooping

    To pick up the keep-sake intended for me.

If a cherub, on pinions of silver descending,

    Had brought me a gem from the fret-work of heaven;

And smiles, with his star-cheering voice sweetly blending,

    The blessing of Tighe had melodiously given;

It had not created a warmer emotion

    Than the present, fair nymphs, I was blest with from you,

Than the shell, from the bright golden sands of the ocean

    Which the emerald waves at your feet gladly threw.

For, indeed, 'tis a sweet and peculiar pleasure

    (And blissful is he who such happiness finds),

To possess but a span of the hour of leisure,

    In elegant, pure, and aerial minds.

DAISY'S SONG

I

THE SUN, WITH HIS GREAT EYE,

Sees not so much as I;

And the moon, all silver-proud,

Might as well be in a cloud.

II

And O the spring – the spring!

I lead the life of a king!

Couch'd in the teeming grass,

I spy each pretty lass.

III

I look where no one dares,

And I stare where no one stares,

And when the night is nigh,

Lambs bleat my lullaby.

John Constable   Sunset Through the Trees: A View on Hampstead Heath

Samuel Palmer SHEEP IN THE SHADE

ENDYMION

A THING OF BEAUTY IS A JOY FOR EVER:

Its loveliness increases; it will never

Pass into nothingness; but still will keep

A bower quiet for us, and a sleep

Full of sweet dreams, and health, and quiet breathing.

Therefore, on every morrow, are we wreathing

A flowery band to bind us to the earth,

Spite of despondence, of the inhuman dearth

Of noble natures, of the gloomy days,

Of all the unhealthy and o'er-darkened ways

Made for our searching: yes, in spite of all,

Some shape of beauty moves away the pall

From our dark spirits. Such the sun, the moon,

Trees old, and young, sprouting a shady boon

For simple sheep; and such are daffodils

With the green world they live in; and clear rills

That for themselves a cooling covert make

'Gainst the hot season; the mid forest brake,

Rich with a sprinkling of fair musk-rose blooms:

And such too is the grandeur of the dooms

We have imagined for the mighty dead;

All lovely tales that we have heard or read:

An endless fountain of immortal drink

Pouring unto us from the heaven's brink.

Extract from ENDYMION

GENTLE BREAMA! BY THE FIRST

Violet young nature nurst,

I will bathe myself with thee,

So you sometimes follow me

To my home, far, far, in west,

Beyond the nimble-wheeled quest

Of the golden-presenc'd sun:

Come with me, o'er tops of trees.

To my fragrant palaces,

Where they ever floating are

Beneath the cherish of a star

Call'd Vesper, who with silver veil

Ever hides his brilliance pale,

Ever gently-drows'd doth keep

Twilight for the Fayes to sleep.

Fear not that your watery hair

Will thirst in drouthy ringlets there:

Clouds of stored summer rains

Thou shalt taste, before the stains

Of the mountain soil they take,

And too unlucent for thee make.

I love thee, crystal Faery, true!

Sooth I am as sick for you!

Joseph Mallord William Turner   MORE PARK c. 1823

Song

Tune – *'Julia to the Wood-Robin'*

Stay, ruby-breasted warbler, stay,
   And let me see thy sparkling eye,
Oh brush not yet the pearl-strung spray
   Nor bow thy pretty head to fly.

Stay while I tell thee, fluttering thing,
   That thou of love an emblem art,
Yes! patient plume thy little wing,
   Whilst I my thoughts to thee impart.

When summer nights the dews bestow,
   And summer suns enrich the day,
Thy notes the blossoms charm to blow,
   Each opes delighted at thy lay.

So when in youth the eye's dark glance
   Speaks pleasure from its circle bright,
The tones of love our joys enhance
   And make superior each delight.

And when bleak storms resistless rove,
   And every rural bliss destroy,
Nought comforts then the leafless grove
   But thy soft note – its only joy –

E'en so the words of love beguile
   When Pleasure's tree no flower bears.
And draw a soft endearing smile
   Amid the gloom and grief of tears.

I HAD A DOVE AND THE SWEET DOVE DIED;

   And I have thought it died of grieving:

O, what could it grieve for? Its feet were tied,

   With a silken thread of my own hand's weaving;

Sweet little red feet! why should you die –

Why should you leave me, sweet dove! why?

You liv'd alone on the forest-tree,

Why, pretty thing! could you not live with me?

I kiss'd you oft and gave you white peas;

Why not live sweetly, as in the green trees?

SHED NO TEAR – O SHED NO TEAR!

The flower will bloom another year.

Weep no more – O weep no more!

Young buds sleep in the root's white core.

Dry your eyes – O dry your eyes,

For I was taught in Paradise

To ease my breast of melodies –

        Shed no tear.

Overhead – look overhead

'Mong the blossoms white and red –

Look up, look up – I flutter now

On this flush pomegranate bough –

See me – 'tis this silvery bill

Ever cures the good man's ill –

Shed no tear – O shed no tear!

The flower will bloom another year.

Adieu – Adieu – I fly, adieu,

I vanish in the heaven's blue –

        Adieu, Adieu!

I

PHYSICIAN NATURE! LET MY SPIRIT BLOOD!

   O ease my heart of verse and let me rest;

Throw me upon thy Tripod, till the flood

   Of stifling numbers ebbs from my full breast.

A theme! a theme! great nature! give a theme;

     Let me begin my dream.

I come – I see thee, as thou standest there,

Beckon me not into the wintry air.

II

Ah! dearest love, sweet home of all my fears,

   And hopes, and joys, and panting miseries, –

To-night, if I may guess, thy beauty wears

     A smile of such delight,

     As brilliant and as bright,

As when with ravished, aching, vassal eyes,

     Lost in soft amaze,

     I gaze, I gaze!

III

Who now, with greedy looks, eats up my feast?

   What stare outfaces now my silver moon!

Ah! keep that hand unravish'd at the least;

     Let, let, the amorous burn –

     But, pr'ythee, do not turn

The current of your heart from me so soon.

     Oh! save, in charity,

     The quickest pulse for me.

IV

Save it for me, sweet love! though music breathe

   Voluptuous visions into the warm air;

Though swimming through the dance's dangerous wreath,

     Be like an April day,

     Smiling and cold and gay,

   A temperate lilly, temperate as fair;

     Then, Heaven! there will be

     A warmer June for me.

George Romney PORTRAIT OF MRS HENRY MAXWELL

William Henry Hunt   SUNDAY MORNING

V

Why, this – you'll say, my Fanny! is not true:
    Put your soft hand upon your snowy side,
Where the heart beats: confess – 'tis nothing new –
        Must not a woman be
        A feather on the sea,
    Sway'd to and fro by every wind and tide?
        Of as uncertain speed
        As blow-ball from the mead?

VI

I know it – and to know it is despair
    To one who loves you as I love, sweet Fanny!
Whose heart goes fluttering for you every where,
        Nor, when away you roam,
        Dare keep its wretched home,
    Love, love alone, has pains severe and many:
        Then, loveliest! keep me free
        From torturing jealousy.

VII

Ah! if you prize my subdued soul above
    The poor, the fading, brief, pride of an hour;
Let none profane my Holy See of love,
        Or with a rude hand break
        The sacramental cake:
    Let none else touch the just new-budded flower;
        If not – may my eyes close,
        Love! on their last repose.

To Autumn

I

SEASON OF MISTS AND MELLOW FRUITFULNESS,

   Close bosom-friend of the maturing sun;

Conspiring with him how to load and bless

   With fruit the vines that round the thatch-eves run;

To bend with apples the moss'd cottage-trees,

   And fill all fruit with ripeness to the core;

     To swell the gourd, and plump the hazel shells

   With a sweet kernel; to set budding more,

And still more, later flowers for the bees,

Until they think warm days will never cease,

     For Summer has o'er brimm'd their clammy cells.

II

Who hath not seen thee oft amid thy store?

   Sometimes whoever seeks abroad may find

Thee sitting careless on a granary floor,

   Thy hair soft-lifted by the winnowing wind;

Or on a half reap'd furrow sound asleep,

   Drows'd with the fume of poppies, while thy hook

     Spares the next swath and all its twined flowers:

And sometimes like a gleaner thou dost keep

   Steady thy laden head across a brook;

   Or by a cyder-press, with patient look,

     Thou watchest the last oozings hours by hours.

III

Where are the songs of Spring? Ay, where are they?

   Think not of them, thou hast thy music too, –

While barred clouds bloom the soft-dying day,

   And touch the stubble-plains with rosy hue;

Then in a wailful choir the small gnats mourn

   Among the river sallows, borne aloft

     Or sinking as the light wind lives or dies;

And full-grown lambs loud bleat from hilly bourn;

   Hedge-crickets sing; and now with treble soft

   The red-breast whistles from a garden-croft;

     And gathering swallows twitter in the skies.

Samuel Palmer   EVENING: A COTTAGER RETURNING HOME GREETED BY HIS CHILDREN *(detail)*

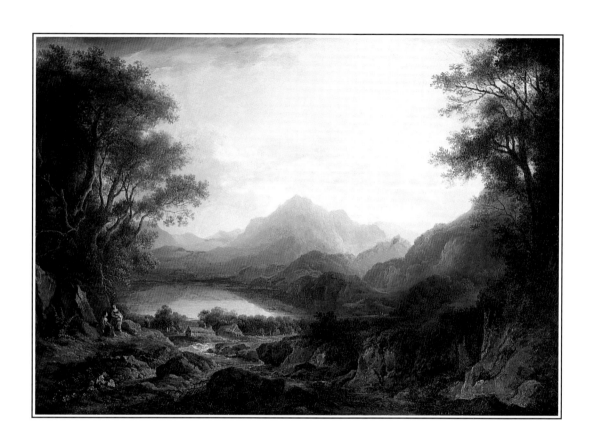

Alexander Nasmyth Loch Lomond

A Ballad

I

O, WHAT CAN AIL THEE, KNIGHT-AT-ARMS,

    Alone and palely loitering?

The sedge has wither'd from the lake,

    And no birds sing.

II

O, what can ail thee, knight-at-arms,

    So haggard and so woe-begone?

The squirrel's granary is full,

    And the harvest's done.

III

I see a lilly on thy brow,

    With anguish moist and fever dew;

And on thy cheeks a fading rose

    Fast withereth too.

IV

I met a lady in the meads,

    Full beautiful – a faery's child,

Her hair was long, her foot was light,

    And her eyes were wild.

V

I made a garland for her head,

    And bracelets too, and fragrant zone;

She look'd at me as she did love,

    And made sweet moan.

VI

I set her on my pacing steed,

    And nothing else saw all day long;

For sidelong would she bend, and sing

    A faery's song.

VII

She found me roots of relish sweet,
    And honey wild, and manna dew,
And sure in language strange she said –
    'I love thee true'.

VIII

She took me to her elfin grot,
    And there she wept and sigh'd full sore,
And there I shut her wild wild eyes
    With kisses four.

IX

And there she lulled me asleep
    And there I dream'd – Ah! woe betide!
The latest dream I ever dream'd
    On the cold hill side.

X

I saw pale kings and princes too,
    Pale warriors, death-pale were they all;
They cried – 'La Belle Dame sans Merci
    Hath thee in thrall!'

XI

I saw their starved lips in the gloam,
    With horrid warning gaped wide,
And I awoke and found me here,
    On the cold hill's side.

XII

And this is why I sojourn here
    Alone and palely loitering,
Though the sedge has wither'd from the lake,
    And no birds sing.

I

MY HEART ACHES, AND A DROWSY
NUMBNESS PAINS

My sense, as though of hemlock I had drunk,
Or emptied some dull opiate to the drains
  One minute past, and Lethe-wards had sunk:
'Tis not through envy of thy happy lot,
  But being too happy in thine happiness, –
    That thou, light-winged Dryad of the trees,
      In some melodious plot
Of beechen green, and shadows numberless,
  Singest of summer in full-throated ease.

II

O, for a draught of vintage! that hath been
  Cool'd a long age in the deep-delved earth,
Tasting of Flora and the country green,
  Dance, and Provençal song, and sunburnt mirth!
O for a beaker full of the warm South,
  Full of the true, the blushful Hippocrene,
    With beaded bubbles winking at the brim,
      And purple-stained mouth;
That I might drink, and leave the world unseen,
  And with thee fade away into the forest dim:

III

Fade far away, dissolve, and quite forget
  What thou among the leaves hast never known,
The weariness, the fever, and the fret
  Here, where men sit and hear each other groan;
Where palsy shakes a few, sad, last gray hairs,
  Where youth grows pale, and spectre-thin, and dies;
    Where but to think is to be full of sorrow
      And leaden-eyed despairs,
Where Beauty cannot keep her lustrous eyes,
  Or new Love pine at them beyond to-morrow.

IV

Away! away! for I will fly to thee,
  Not charioted by Bacchus and his pards,
But on the viewless wings of Poesy,
  Though the dull brain perplexes and retards:
Already with thee! tender is the night,
  And haply the Queen-Moon is on her throne,
    Cluster'd around by all her starry Fays;
      But here there is no light,
Save what from heaven is with the breezes blown
  Through verdurous glooms and winding mossy ways.

V

I cannot see what flowers are at my feet,
  Nor what soft incense hangs upon the boughs,
But, in embalmed darkness, guess each sweet
  Wherewith the seasonable month endows
The grass, the thicket, and the fruit-tree wild;
  White hawthorn, and the pastoral eglantine;
    Fast fading violets cover'd up in leaves;
      And mid-May's eldest child,
  The coming musk-rose, full of dewy wine,
    The murmurous haunt of flies on summer eves.

VI

Darkling I listen; and, for many a time
  I have been half in love with easeful Death,
Call'd him soft names in many a mused rhyme,
  To take into the air my quiet breath;
Now more than ever seems it rich to die,
  To cease upon the midnight with no pain,
    While thou art pouring forth thy soul abroad
      In such an ecstasy!
  Still wouldst thou sing, and I have ears in vain –
    To thy high requiem become a sod.

VII

Thou wast not born for death, immortal Bird!
  No hungry generations tread thee down;
The voice I hear this passing night was heard
  In ancient days by emperor and clown:
Perhaps the self-same song that found a path
  Through the sad heart of Ruth, when, sick for home,
    She stood in tears amid the alien corn;
      The same that oft-times hath
  Charm'd magic casements, opening on the foam
    Of perilous seas, in faery lands forlorn.

VIII

Forlorn! the very word is like a bell
  To toll me back from thee to my sole self!
Adieu! the fancy cannot cheat so well
  As she is fam'd to do, deceiving elf.
Adieu! adieu! thy plaintive anthem fades
  Past the near meadows, over the still stream,
    Up the hill-side; and now 'tis buried deep
      In the next valley-glades:
  Was it a vision, or a waking dream?
    Fled is that music: — Do I wake or sleep?

Joseph Severn   Keats Listening to the Nightingale on Hampstead Heath

John Constable   Hove Beach

IT KEEPS ETERNAL WHISPERINGS AROUND

Desolate shores, and with its mighty swell

Gluts twice ten thousand Caverns, till the spell

Of Hecate leaves them their old shadowy sound.

Often 'tis in such gentle temper found,

That scarcely will the very smallest shell

Be mov'd for days from where it sometime fell,

When last the winds of Heaven were unbound.

Oh ye! who have your eye-balls vex'd and tir'd,

Feast them upon the wideness of the Sea;

Oh ye! whose ears are dinn'd with uproar rude,

Or fed too much with cloying melody –

Sit ye near some old Cavern's Mouth and brood,

Until ye start, as if the sea-nymphs quir'd!

O H HOW I LOVE, ON A FAIR SUMMER'S EVE,

When streams of light pour down the golden west,

And on the balmy zephyrs tranquil rest

The silver clouds, far – far away to leave

All meaner thoughts, and take a sweet reprieve

From little cares; to find, with easy quest,

A fragrant wild, with Nature's beauty drest,

And there into delight my soul deceive.

There warm my breast with patriotic lore,

Musing on Milton's fate – on Sydney's bier –

Till their stern forms before my mind arise:

Perhaps on wing of Poesy upsoar,

Full often dropping a delicious tear,

When some melodious sorrow spells mine eyes.

Samuel Palmer   Eventide

TIME'S SEA HATH BEEN FIVE YEARS AT ITS SLOW EBB,

Long hours have to and fro let creep the sand,

Since I was tangled in thy beauty's web,

And snared by the ungloving of thine hand.

And yet I never look on midnight sky,

But I behold thine eyes' well memory'd light;

I cannot look upon the rose's dye,

But to thy cheek my soul doth take its flight.

I cannot look on any budding flower,

But my fond ear, in fancy at thy lips

And hearkening for a love-sound, doth devour

Its sweets in the wrong sense: – Thou dost eclipse

Every delight with sweet remembering,

And grief unto my darling joys dost bring.

Thomas Gainsborough   MRS RICHARD BRINSLEY SHERIDAN

O SOFT EMBALMER OF THE STILL MIDNIGHT,

    Shutting, with careful fingers and benign,

Our gloom-pleas'd eyes, embower'd from the light,

    Enshaded in forgetfulness divine:

O soothest Sleep! if so it please thee, close

    In midst of this thine hymn my willing eyes,

Or wait the amen, ere thy poppy throws

    Around my bed its lulling charities.

Then save me, or the passed day will shine

Upon my pillow, breeding many woes, –

    Save me from curious Conscience, that still lords

Its strength for darkness, burrowing like a mole;

    Turn the key deftly in the oiled wards,

And seal the hushed Casket of my Soul.

Samuel Palmer   THE SLEEPING SHEPHERD, MORNING

AS HERMES ONCE TOOK TO HIS FEATHERS LIGHT,

    When lulled Argus, baffled, swoon'd and slept,

So on a Delphic reed, my idle spright,

    So play'd, so charm'd so conquer'd, so bereft

The dragon-world of all its hundred eyes:

    And, seeing it asleep, so fled away,

Not to pure Ida with its snow-cold skies,

    Nor unto Tempe, where Jove griev'd that day;

But to that second circle of sad hell,

    Where in the gust, the whirlwind, and the flaw

Of rain and hail-stones, lovers need not tell

Their sorrows – pale were the sweet lips I saw,

Pale were the lips I kiss'd, and fair the form

I floated with, about that melancholy storm.

John Linnell THE LAST GLEAM BEFORE THE STORM

John Martin   Landscape at Dusk

Sonnet   Bright Star

Written on a Blank Page in Shakespeare's Poems, facing 'A Lover's
Complaint.'

Bright star! would I were steadfast as thou art –
 Not in lone splendour hung aloft the night
And watching, with eternal lids apart,
 Like nature's patient, sleepless Eremite,
The moving waters at their priestlike task
 Of pure ablution round earth's human shores,
Or gazing on the new soft fallen mask
 Of snow upon the mountains and the moors –
No – yet still steadfast, still unchangeable,
 Pillow'd upon my fair love's ripening breast,
To feel for ever its soft fall and swell,
 Awake for ever in a sweet unrest,
Still, still to hear her tender-taken breath,
And so live ever – or else swoon to death.

O **SOLITUDE! IF I MUST WITH THEE DWELL,**

Let it not be among the jumbled heap

Of murky buildings; climb with me the steep, –

Nature's observatory – whence the dell,

Its flowery slopes, its river's crystal swell,

May seem a span; let me thy vigils keep

'Mongst boughs pavillion'd, where the deer's swift leap

Startles the wild bee from the fox-glove bell.

But though I'll gladly trace these scenes with thee,

Yet the sweet converse of an innocent mind,

Whose words are images of thoughts refin'd,

Is my soul's pleasure; and it sure must be

Almost the highest bliss of human-kind,

When to thy haunts two kindred spirits flee.

William Daniel   DEER IN A WOODED LANDSCAPE

Samuel Palmer   THE BELLMAN

K EEN, FITFUL GUSTS ARE WHISP'RING HERE AND THERE

Among the bushes half leafless, and dry;

The stars look very cold about the sky,

And I have many miles on foot to fare.

Yet feel I little of the cool bleak air,

Or of the dead leaves rustling drearily,

Or of those silver lamps that burn on high,

Or of the distance from home's pleasant lair:

For I am brimfull of the friendliness

That in a little cottage I have found:

Of fair-hair'd Milton's eloquent distress,

And all his love for gentle Lycid drown'd;

Of lovely Laura in her light green dress,

And faithful Petrarch gloriously crown'd.

TO ONE WHO HAS BEEN LONG IN CITY PENT,

'Tis very sweet to look into the fair

And open face of heaven, – to breathe a prayer

Full in the smile of the blue firmament.

Who is more happy, when, with heart's content,

Fatigued he sinks into some pleasant lair

Of wavy grass, and reads a debonair

And gentle tale of love and languishment?

Returning home at evening, with an ear

Catching the notes of Philomel, – an eye

Watching the sailing cloudlet's bright career,

He mourns that day so soon has glided by:

E'en like the passage of an angel's tear

That falls through the clear ether silently.

Alexander Nasmyth   A View at Paticroft

John Constable STUDY OF SEA AND SKY

RITTEN IN ANSWER TO A SONNET ENDING THUS:

DARK EYES ARE DEARER FAR

THAN THOSE THAT MOCK THE HYACINTHINE BELL –

By J. H. REYNOLDS

B LUE! 'TIS THE LIFE OF HEAVEN, – THE DOMAIN
 Of Cynthia, – the wide palace of the sun –
The tent of Hesperus, and all his train, –
 The bosomer of clouds, gold, grey and dun.
Blue! 'Tis the life of waters: – Ocean
 And all its vassal streams, pools numberless,
May rage, and foam, and fret, but never can
 Subside, if not to dark blue nativeness.
Blue! Gentle cousin of the forest-green,
 Married to green in all the sweetest flowers, –
Forget-me-not, – the Blue bell, – and, that Queen
 Of secrecy, the Violet: what strange powers
Hast thou, as a mere shadow! But how great,
When in an Eye thou art, alive with fate!

FRAGMENT

'UNDER THE FLAG

OF EACH HIS FACTION, THEY TO BATTLE BRING

THEIR EMBRYON ATOMS.' MILTON

WELCOME JOY, AND WELCOME SORROW,

   Lethe's weed and Hermes' feather;

Come to-day, and come to-morrow,

   I do love you both together!

   I love to mark sad faces in fair weather;

And hear a merry laugh amid the thunder;

   Fair and foul I love together.

Meadows sweet where flames are under,

And a giggle at a wonder;

Visage sage at pantomime;

Funeral, and steeple-chime;

Infant playing with a skull;

Morning fair, and shipwreck'd hull;

Nightshade with the woodbine kissing;

Serpents in red roses hissing;

Cleopatra regal-dress'd

With the aspic at her breast;

Dancing music, music sad,

Both together, sane and mad;

Muses bright and muses pale;

Sombre Saturn, Momus hale; –

Laugh and sigh, and laugh again;

Oh the sweetness of the pain!

Muses bright and muses pale,

Bare your faces of the veil;

Let me see; and let me write

Of the day, and of the night –

Both together: – let me slake

All my thirst for sweet heart-ache!

Let my bower be of yew,

Interwreath'd with myrtles new;

Pines and lime-trees full in bloom,

And my couch a low grass tomb.

Anonymous [early 19th Century]   LANDSCAPE AT HARVEST

Samuel Palmer   THE FURZE FIELD

THE POETRY OF EARTH IS NEVER DEAD:

When all the birds are faint with the hot sun,

And hide in cooling trees, a voice will run

From hedge to hedge about the new-mown mead;

That is the Grasshopper's – he takes the lead

In summer luxury, – he has never done

With his delights; for when tired out with fun

He rests at ease beneath some pleasant weed.

The poetry of earth is ceasing never:

On a lone winter evening, when the frost

Has wrought a silence, from the stove there shrills

The Cricket's song, in warmth increasing ever,

And seems to one in drowsiness half lost,

The Grasshopper's among some grassy hills.

SEE, **THE SHIP IN THE BAY IS RIDING,**

Dearest Ellen, I go from thee;

Boldly go, in thy love confiding,

Over the deep and trackless sea: –

When thy dear form no longer is near me,

This soothing thought shall at midnight chear me;

'My love is breathing a prayer for me'. –

When the thunder of war is roaring,

When the bullets around me fly,

When the rage of the tempest pouring

Bends the billowy sea and sky,

Yet shall my heart, to fear a stranger,

Cherish its fondest hopes for thee: –

This dear reflection disarming danger,

'My love is breathing a prayer for me'.

Joseph Mallord William Turner   PLYMOUTH HARBOUR

George Romney 'PSYCHE IN A WOOD'

O **GODDESS! HEAR THESE TUNELESS**

    NUMBERS, WRUNG

By sweet enforcement and remembrance dear,

And pardon that thy secrets should be sung

    Even into thine own soft-conched ear:

Surely I dreamt to-day, or did I see

    The winged Psyche with awaken'd eyes?

I wander'd in a forest thoughtlessly,

    And, on the sudden, fainting with surprise,

Saw two fair creatures, couched side by side

    In deepest grass, beneath the whisp'ring roof

Of leaves and trembled blossoms, where there ran

      A brooklet, scarce espied:

'Mid hush'd, cool-rooted flowers, fragrant-eyed,

    Blue, silver-white, and budded Tyrian,

They lay calm-breathing on the bedded grass;

    Their arms embraced, and their pinions too;

    Their lips touch'd not, but had not bid adieu,

As if disjoined by soft-handed slumber,

And ready still past kisses to outnumber

    At tender eye-dawn of aurorean love:

    The winged boy I knew;

But who was thou, O happy, happy dove?

    His Psyche true!

O latest born and loveliest vision far

    Of all Olympus' faded hierarchy!

Fairer than Phoebe's sapphire-region'd star,

    Or Vesper, amorous glow-worm of the sky;

Fairer than these, though temple thou has none,

    Nor altar heap'd with flowers;

Nor virgin-choir to make delicious moan

    Upon the midnight hours;

No voice, no lute, no pipe, no incense sweet

    From chain-swung censer teeming;

No shrine, no grove, no oracle, no heat

    Of pale-mouth'd prophet dreaming.

O brightest! though too late for antique vows,

    Too, too late for the fond believing lyre,

When holy were the haunted forest boughs,
      Holy the air, the water, and the fire;
Yet even in these days so far retir'd
      From happy pieties, thy lucent fans,
      Fluttering among the faint Olympians,
I see, and sing, by my own eyes inspired.
So let me be thy choir, and make a moan
      Upon the midnight hours;
Thy voice, thy lute, thy pipe, thy incense sweet
      From swinged censer teeming;
Thy shrine, thy grove, thy oracle, thy heat
      Of pale-mouth'd prophet dreaming.

Yes, I will be thy priest, and build a fane
      In some untrodden region of my mind,
Where branched thoughts, new grown with pleasant
      pain,
      Instead of pines shall murmur in the wind:
Far, far around shall those dark-cluster'd trees
      Fledge the wild-ridged mountains steep by steep;
And there by zephyrs, streams, and birds, and bees,

The moss-lain Dryads shall be lull'd to sleep;
And in the midst of this wide quietness
A rosy sanctuary will I dress
With the wreath'd trellis of a working brain,
      With buds, and bells, and stars without a name,
With all the gardener Fancy e'er could feign,
      Who breeding flowers, will never breed the same:
And there shall be for thee all soft delight
      That shadowy thought can win,
A bright torch, and a casement ope at night,
      To let the warm Love in!

ODE ON INDOLENCE

'THEY TOIL NOT, NEITHER DO THEY SPIN.'

ONE MORN BEFORE ME WERE THREE FIGURES SEEN,

With bowed necks, and joined hands, side-faced;

And one behind the other stepp'd serene,

In placid sandals, and in white robes graced;

They pass'd, like figures on a marble urn,

When shifted round to see the other side;

They came again; as when the urn once more

Is shifted round, the first seen shades return;

And they were strange to me, as may betide

With vases, to one deep in Phidian lore.

How is it, Shadows! that I knew ye not?

How came ye muffled in so hush a masque?

Was it a silent deep-disguised plot

To steal away, and leave without a task

My idle days? Ripe was the drowsy hour;

The blissful cloud of summer-indolence

Benumb'd my eyes; my pulse grew less and less;

Pain had no sting, and pleasure's wreath no flower:

O, why did ye not melt, and leave my sense

Unhaunted quite of all but – nothingness?

A third time came they by; – alas! wherefore?

My sleep had been embroider'd with dim dreams;

My soul had been a lawn besprinkled o'er

With flowers, and stirring shades, and baffled beams:

The morn was clouded, but no shower fell,

Tho' in her lids hung the sweet tears of May;

The open casement press'd a new-leav'd vine,

Let in the budding warmth and throstle's lay;

O Shadows! 'twas a time to bid farewell!

Upon your skirts had fallen no tears of mine.

A third time pass'd they by, and, passing, turn'd

Each one the face a moment whiles to me;

Then faded, and to follow them I burn'd

And ached for wings because I knew the three;

The first was a fair Maid, and Love her name;

The second was Ambition, pale of cheek

And ever watchful with fatigued eye;

The last, whom I love more, the more of blame

Is heap'd upon her, maiden most unmeek, –

I knew to be my demon Poesy.

They faded, and, forsooth! I wanted wings:
O folly! What is Love! and where is it?
And for that poor Ambition – it springs
From a man's little heart's short fever-fit;
For Poesy! – no, – she has not a joy, –
At least for me, – so sweet as drowsy noons,
And evenings steep'd in honied indolence;
O, for an age so shelter'd from annoy,
That I may never know how change the moons,
Or hear the voice of busy common-sense!

So, ye three Ghosts, adieu! Ye cannot raise
My head cool-bedded in the flowery grass;
For I would not be dieted with praise,
A pet-lamb in a sentimental farce!
Fade softly from my eyes, and be once more
In masque-like figures on the dreamy urn;
Farewell! I yet have visions for the night,
And for the day faint visions there is store;
Vanish, ye Phantoms! from my idle spright,
Into the clouds, and never more return!

George Arnald NARCISSUS AND ECHO

O COME, DEAREST EMMA, THE ROSE IS FULL BLOWN,

The riches of Flora are lavishly strown,

The air is all softness, and crystal the streams,

The West is resplendently clothed in beams.

O come! let us haste to the freshening shades,

The quaintly carv'd seats, and the opening glades;

Where the faeries are chanting their evening hymns,

And in the last sun-beam the sylph lightly swims.

And when thou art weary I'll find thee a bed,

Of mosses and flowers to pillow thy head:

There, beauteous Emma, I'll sit at thy feet,

While my story of love I enraptur'd repeat.

So fondly I'll breathe, and so softly I'll sigh,

Thou wilt think that some amorous Zephyr is nigh:

Yet no – as I breathe I will press thy fair knee,

And then thou wilt know that the sigh comes from me.

Then why dearest girl should we lose all these blisses?

That mortal's a fool who such happiness misses:

So smile acquiescence, and give me thy hand,

With love-looking eye, and with voice sweetly bland.

Thomas Creswick THE STILE

I

IN A DREAR-NIGHTED DECEMBER,
     Too happy, happy tree,
Thy Branches ne'er remember
     Their green felicity:
     The north cannot undo them,
     With a sleety whistle through them;
     Nor frozen thawings glue them
          From budding at the prime.

II

In a drear-nighted December,
     Too happy, happy Brook,
Thy bubblings ne'er remember
     Apollo's summer look;
     But with a sweet forgetting,
     They stay their crystal fretting,
     Never, never petting
          About the frozen time.

III

Ah! would 'twere so with many
     A gentle girl and boy!
But were there ever any
     Writh'd not of passed joy?
     The feel of not to feel it,
     When there is none to heal it,
     Nor numbed sense to steel it,
          Was never said in rhyme.

Joseph Mallord William Turner   FROSTY MORNING

OLD MEG

OLD MEG SHE WAS A GIPSEY,
  And liv'd upon the Moors;
Her bed it was the brown heath turf,
  And her house was out of doors.

Her apples were swart blackberries,
  Her currants, pods o' broom;
Her wine was dew of the wild white rose,
  Her book a churchyard tomb.

Her Brothers were the craggy hills,
  Her Sisters larchen trees;
Alone with her great family
  She liv'd as she did please.

No breakfast had she many a morn,
  No dinner many a noon,
And, 'stead of supper, she would stare
  Full hard against the Moon.

But every morn, of woodbine fresh
  She made her garlanding,
And, every night, the dark glen Yew
  She wove, and she would sing.

And with her fingers, old and brown,
  She plaited Mats o' Rushes,
And gave them to the Cottagers
  She met among the Bushes.

Old Meg was brave as Margaret Queen
  And tall as Amazon;
An old red blanket cloak she wore,
  A chip hat had she on.
God rest her aged bones somewhere!
  She died full long agone!

George Morland   WINDY DAY

Thomas Gainsborough Landscape: Children and Cattle

I

WHERE BE YE GOING, YOU DEVON MAID?

And what have ye there in the Basket?

Ye tight little fairy just fresh from the dairy,

Will ye give me some cream if I ask it?

III

I love your hills, and I love your dales,

And I love your flocks a-bleating –

But O, on the heather to lie together,

With both our hearts a-beating!

II

I love your Meads, and I love your flowers,

And I love your junkets mainly,

But 'hind the door I love kissing more,

O look not so disdainly.

IV

I'll put your Basket all safe in a nook,

Your shawl I hang up on the willow,

And we will sigh in the daisy's eye

And kiss on a grass green pillow.

I

NO, NO, GO NOT TO LETHE, NEITHER TWIST
   Wolf's-bane, tight-rooted, for its poisonous wine;
Nor suffer thy pale forehead to be kiss'd
   By nightshade, ruby grape of Proserpine;
Make not your rosary of yew-berries,
   Nor let the beetle, nor the death-moth be
      Your mournful Psyche, nor the downy owl
A partner in your sorrow's mysteries;
   For shade to shade will come too drowsily,
      And drown the wakeful anguish of the soul.

II

But when the melancholy fit shall fall
   Sudden from heaven like a weeping cloud,
That fosters the droop-headed flowers all,
   And hides the green hill in an April shroud;
Then glut thy sorrow on a morning rose,
   Or on the rainbow of the salt sand-wave,
      Or on the wealth of globed peonies;
Or if thy mistress some rich anger shows,
   Emprison her soft hand, and let her rave,
      And feed deep, deep upon her peerless eyes.

III

She dwells with Beauty – Beauty that must die;
   And Joy, whose hand is ever at his lips
Bidding adieu; and aching Pleasure nigh,
   Turning to poison while the bee-mouth sips:
Ay, in the very temple of Delight
   Veil'd Melancholy has her sovran shrine,
      Though seen of none save him whose
         strenuous tongue
Can burst Joy's grape against his palate fine;
   His soul shall taste the sadness of her might,
      And be among her cloudy trophies hung.

Samuel Palmer   THE HARVEST MOON: FOR 'A PASTORAL SCENE' c.1831-2

Ode on a Grecian Urn

I

THOU STILL UNRAVISH'D BRIDE OF QUIETNESS,
Thou foster-child of silence and slow time,
Sylvan historian, who canst thus express
A flowery tale more sweetly than our rhyme:
What leaf-fring'd legend haunts about thy shape
Of deities or mortals, or of both,
In Tempe or the dales of Arcady?
What men or gods are these? What maidens loth?
What mad pursuit? What struggle to escape?
What pipes and timbrels? What wild ecstasy?

II

Heard melodies are sweet, but those unheard
Are sweeter; therefore, ye soft pipes, play on;
Not to the sensual ear, but, more endear'd,
Pipe to the spirit ditties of no tone:
Fair youth, beneath the trees, thou canst not leave
Thy song, nor ever can those trees be bare;
Bold Lover, never, never canst thou kiss,
Though winning near the goal – yet, do not grieve;
She cannot fade, though thou hast not thy bliss,
For ever wilt thou love, and she be fair!

III

Ah, happy, happy boughs! that cannot shed
Your leaves, nor ever bid the Spring adieu;
And, happy melodist, unwearied,
For ever piping songs for ever new;
More happy love! more happy, happy love!
For ever warm and still to be enjoy'd,
For ever panting, and for ever young;
All breathing human passion far above,
That leaves a heart high-sorrowful and cloy'd,
A burning forehead, and a parching tongue.

IV

Who are these coming to the sacrifice?
　To what green altar, O mysterious priest,
Lead'st thou that heifer lowing at the skies,
　And all her silken flanks with garlands drest?
What little town by river or sea shore,
　Or mountain-built with peaceful citadel,
　　Is emptied of this folk, this pious morn?
And, little town, thy streets for evermore
　Will silent be; and not a soul to tell
　　Why thou art desolate, can e'er return.

V

O Attic shape! Fair attitude! with brede
　Of marble men and maidens overwrought,
With forest branches and the trodden weed;
　Thou, silent form, dost tease us out of thought
As doth eternity: Cold Pastoral!
　When old age shall this generation waste,
　　Thou shalt remain, in midst of other woe
Than ours, a friend to man, to whom thou say'st,
　Beauty is truth, truth beauty, – that is all
　　Ye know on earth, and all ye need to know.

SWEET, SWEET IS THE GREETING OF EYES

SWEET, SWEET IS THE GREETING OF EYES,
And sweet is the voice in its greeting,
When Adieux have grown old and goodbyes
Fade away where old Time is retreating

Warm the nerve of a welcoming hand,
And earnest a Kiss on the Brow,
When we meet over sea and o'er Land
Where Furrows are new to the Plough.

As i lay in my bed slepe full unmete

Was unto me, but why that i ne might

Rest i ne wist, for there n'as erthly wight

[As i suppose] had more of hertis ese

Than i, for i n'ad sicknesse nor disese.

Chaucer

WHAT IS MORE GENTLE THAN A WIND IN SUMMER?

What is more soothing than the pretty hummer

That stays one moment in an open flower,

And buzzes cheerily from bower to bower?

What is more tranquil than a musk-rose blowing

In a green island, far from all men's knowing?

More healthful than the leafiness of dales?

More secret than a nest of nightingales?

More serene than Cordelia's countenance?

More full of visions than a high romance?

What, but thee Sleep? Soft closer of our eyes!

Low murmurer of tender lullabies!

Light hoverer around our happy pillows!

Wreather of poppy buds, and weeping willows!

Silent entangler of a beauty's tresses!

Most happy listener! when the morning blesses

Thee for enlivening all the cheerful eyes

That glance so brightly at the new sun-rise.

But what is higher beyond thought than thee?

Fresher than berries of a mountain tree?

More strange, more beautiful, more smooth, more regal,

Than wings of swans, than doves, than dim-seen eagle?

What is it? And to what shall I compare it?

It has a glory, and naught else can share it:

The thought thereof is awful, sweet, and holy,

Chasing away all worldiness and folly;

Coming sometimes like fearful claps of thunder,

Or the low rumblings earth's regions under;

And sometimes like a gentle whispering

Andrew Nicholl WATERFORD

Of all the secrets of some wond'rous thing
That breathes about us in the vacant air;
So that we look around with prying stare,
Perhaps to see shapes of light, aerial limning,
And catch soft floatings from a faint-heard hymning;
To see the laurel wreath, on high suspended,
That is to crown our name when life is ended.
Sometimes it gives a glory to the voice,
And from the heart up-springs, 'Rejoice! rejoice!'
Sounds which will reach the Framer of all things,
And die away in ardent mutterings.

No one who once the glorious sun has seen,
And all the clouds, and felt his bosom clean
For his great Maker's presence, but must know
What 'tis I mean, and feel his being glow:
Therefore no insult will I give his spirit,
By telling what he sees from native merit.

O Poesy! for thee I hold my pen
That am not yet a glorious denizen
Of thy wide heaven – Should I rather kneel
Upon some mountain-top until I feel
A glowing splendour round about me hung,
An echo back the voice of thine own tongue?

Extract from SLEEP AND POETRY

CAT! WHO HAST PAST THY GRAND CLIMACTERIC,

How many mice and Rats hast in thy days

Destroy'd – how many tit bits stolen? Gaze

With those bright languid segments green and prick

Those velvet ears – but pr'ythee do not stick

Thy latent talons in me – and upraise

Thy gentle mew – and tell me all thy frays

Of Fish and Mice, and Rats and tender chick.

Nay look not down, nor lick thy dainty wrists –

For all the weezy Asthma, – and for all

Thy tail's tip is nicked off – and though the fists

Of many a Maid have given thee many a maul,

Still is that fur as soft as when the lists

In youth thou enter'dst on glass-bottled wall.

HYPERION

BOOK I

DEEP IN THE SHADY SADNESS OF A VALE

Far sunken from the healthy breath of morn,

Far from the fiery noon, and eve's one star,

Sat gray-hair'd Saturn, quiet as a stone,

Still as the silence round about his lair;

Forest on forest hung above his head

Like cloud on cloud. No stir of air was there,

Not so much life as on a summer's day

Robs not one light seed from the feather'd grass,

But where the dead leaf fell, there did it rest.

A stream went voiceless by, still deadened more

By reason of his fallen divinity

Spreading a shade; the naiad 'mid her reeds

Press'd her cold finger closer to her lips.

    Along the margin-sand large foot-marks went,

No further than to where his feet had stray'd,

And slept there since. Upon the sodden ground

His old right hand lay nerveless, listless, dead,

Unsceptred: and his realmless eyes were closed;

While his bow'd head seem'd list'ning to the Earth,

His ancient mother, for some comfort yet.

    It seem'd no force could wake him from his place;

But there came one, who with a kindred hand

Touch'd his wide shoulders, after bending low

With reverence, though to one who knew it not.

She was a Goddess of the infant world;

By her in stature the tall Amazon

Had stood a pigmy's height: she would have ta'en

Achilles by the hair and bent his neck;

Or with a finger stay'd Ixion's wheel.

Her face was large as that of Memphian sphinx,

Pedestal'd haply in a palace court,

When sages look'd to Egypt for their lore.

But oh! how unlike marble was that face:

How beautiful, if sorrow had not made

Sorrow more beautiful than Beauty's self.

John Ruskin   STUDY OF TREES WITH A HILLSIDE TOWN

Extract from HYPERION

Acknowledgements

Ackermann and Johnson Ltd, London/Bridgeman Art Library, *page 83*.

Christie's Images, *pages 2, 13, 27, 28, 36, 39, 71, 77, 91 and 94*.

Christie's London/Bridgeman Art Library, *pages 17, 35, 59, 64*.

Fitzwilliam Museum, Cambridge, *page 52*.

Gavin Graham Gallery/Bridgeman Art Library, *page 18*.

Mellon Collection, National Gallery of Art, Washington/Bridgeman Art Library, *page 50*.

Roy Miles Gallery/Bridgeman Art Library, *page 60*.

National Gallery, London, *page 24*.

National Portrait Gallery, London, *page 6*.

The National Trust Photographic Library (Jonathon Gibson)/Fenton House, Hampstead, *page 67*.

The National Trust Photographic Library (Derrick E. Witty)/Petworth House, *page 84*.

Sotheby's, London, *pages 21, 40, 56, 63, 72 and cover*.

Tate Gallery, London, *pages 31, 78, 81 and 87*.

Victoria and Albert Museum, London/Bridgeman Art Library, *pages 14, 46 and 68*.

Walker Art Gallery, (Board of Trustees of the National Museums and Galleries on Merseyside), Liverpool, *page 55*.

Christopher Wood Gallery, London/Bridgeman Art Library, *page 49*.

Woodmansterne Ltd, (Jeremy Marks), *page 45*.

PICTURE RESEARCH: GABRIELLE ALLEN